To Jacki
Best Wishes
Fred Hilliers 1995

Further down the back

the

Best Wishes
Fred Hillier

Further down the back

A Celebration of the Great Australian Dunny

FRED HILLIER

HarperCollins*Publishers*

HarperCollins_Publishers_

25 Ryde Road, Pymble, Sydney NSW 2073, Australia
31 View Road, Glenfield, Auckland 10, New Zealand

First published in Australia in 1993

National Library of Australia
Cataloguing-in-Publication data:

Hillier, Fred
Further down the back.

Bibliography.
ISBN 0 7322 5033 1.
1. Outhouses — Australia. I. Title
392.3600994

Printed by Macpherson's Print Group, Victoria.

9 8 7 6 5 4 3 2 1
96 95 94 93

*This book is dedicated to all those who can remember
and to my family and friends who have tolerated
my eccentricities in matters of the loo.*

A loo built from granite, brick, earth, wood and iron in Molong, NSW.

Contents

ACKNOWLEDGMENTS

Phillip Adams, Jim Foster, *Newbury Weekly News,* New Orchard Editions, Vicki Mall, Colin Shakespeare, Mrs Amiott, Will Pearce, Great Western Railway, Stan Richards, Dawn Dicker, Adeline Beltzo, *Sydney Morning Herald,* Terry Stewart (NSW Water Board), Pro Hart, Peg Shapcott, Kathleen Stewart, Betty Charlton, The Corporation for Jefferson's Poplar Forest, Gertrude Skinner, Marie Hombsch, Diane White, Bob Thompson, Glenise Pettersen, Myrtle Thornton, Kylie Bettridge, Penguin Books Ltd Australia for permission to reproduce an excerpt from *A Fortunate Life* by A. B. Facey, the *Washington Post,* Grahame Watt, Max Fatchen, the *Adelaide Advertiser,* Nancy Dold, Eric Jolliffe, Smoky Dawson, and *Northern Daily Leader*, Tamworth.

A thankyou must go to Ian Richards (who has kept our business wheels turning while I've been otherwise engaged) and special thanks to all those people who, over the years, have related stories and sent me newspaper clippings and photographs. In addition, I want to thank the owners of outhouses that I have photographed for retaining these icons of Australian culture. These people are the unsung heroes of privyology.

Here is a not-so-flash Aussie down the back. It's not built too well — one good blow would knock it down!

Introduction

As a child I lived in Sydney and as far as I was concerned if one had to live in a city it was necessary to have a back lane. A back lane was kids' territory — a place to meet, play cricket and to generally get up to mischief. In the 1950s my back lane had a certain charm. There were choko, passionfruit and bean vines hanging over fences and passers-by could help themselves to the fruit. In many back lanes boundary fences had wooden palings with cracks just wide enough so kids could spy on the activities of residents in their backyards. On one of my spying sorties I came to realise for the first time that the lavatory could be used for more than the call of nature. On that occasion, I peered through a crack and saw a neighbour sitting on the 'dunny' with his trousers down, reading the Saturday horseracing guide. On the bench seat next to him was an old portable valve radio broadcasting the race results. I later learnt that if it was a hot day the dunny punter would retrieve a bottle of beer from the overhead cistern where it was placed to keep cool.

Another dunny experience from my childhood that has remained imprinted on my mind occurred at a weekender my parents took me to regularly in the Blue Mountains, west of Sydney. My father was a plumber and had a way with corrugated iron. He fashioned a dunny out of an old rainwater tank which had no fancy accoutrements, only a four-gallon (25-litre) drum with a rough wooden seat. I was petrified when a large black snake entered the dunny and glided around the periphery while I stood balanced on the seat of the can.

This is a pretty flash Aussie down the back. Hope there's a chain and hook on the inside too!

Once the 'weekender days' were gone outhouses did not play a part in my life (other than to satisfy calls of nature) until the mid-1970s when, working as an engineer surveyor on properties in the west of New South Wales, I began to take an interest in early pioneering building methods. I was fascinated by the improvisation skills of the pioneers and these were especially evident when it came to building outhouses. In 1974 I left my surveying job and began manipulating clay, firstly making ceramic figurines and then, when seeking a diversion, miniature clay dunnies and farm buildings. One of the most famous ceramic pieces I have made was a reproduction of a portion of the back lanes of Broken Hill, New South Wales. There, dunnies back on to the lanes so the sanno-man could access the cans from the rear. No two loos were the same, an undeniable ceramic artist's delight.

Another highlight was being commissioned by the workers of a Tamworth health department to make a section of the back lane outhouses as a retirement gift for the head of the department. On the night of the presentation dinner the Master of Ceremonies said, 'I know of no other person in Tamworth who could have such appropriate letters behind his name — S.H.I.T., for Senior Health Inspector, Tamworth.' Very fitting indeed!

A beautiful Victorian pottery pedestal in Keswick, England. Photo courtesy of Bob Thompson.

Me outside my specially fitted-out visitor's dunny. Photo courtesy of Northern Daily Leader, Tamworth.

So popular have my ceramics become that at an exhibition in Sydney the media discovered me. When my efforts hit the air waves the public responded with their dunny stories and so material was obtained for my first book on the dunny, *Down the Back — the Era of the Outhouse* and now this book, *Further Down the Back*.

Australian author and radio presenter Phillip Adams saw the subject whimsically when writing for the *Bulletin* in 1983.

May It Never Shrink From Our Sight

The South Americans shrink heads. The Japanese shrink trees. The *Reader's Digest* shrinks novels. And Fred Hillier shrinks dunnies.

His little loos, his bonsai'd bogs, his Lilliputian lavs, all lovingly sculptured in dung-coloured clay, tug at the heart and tease the eye. They now share a space on my shelves with pre-dynastic pots from Egypt, the odd Grecian urn and look every bit as ancient. And, given the ability of ceramics to scoff at the centuries, I've no doubt that, in a few thousand years, they'll be unearthed by archaeologists who'll come to one of two conclusions: that Australians worshipped the sanitary version of the sentry box or that we lived in very small houses.

In England my activities were reported by the *Newbury Weekly News* in June 1984.

Intrepid Aussie Tracks Down a Thatched Loo

Unlike most visitors to this part of the world, Australian artist and sculptor Fred Hillier is not touring the usual crop of country houses and museums.

Not for him the cultural delights of Donnington Castle, Littlecote House, nor any of the other major tourist attractions in the area.

Instead, Mr Hillier is scouring the country in search of its smallest rooms — and he's discovered in the process that as far as the British are concerned, the loo is taboo.

The media is obsessed with stories relating to the loo, maybe because the subject is light-hearted and humorous. For me, dunnies, outhouses, loos, toilets — whatever you like to call them — are part of our social history and the folklore associated with them needs to be recorded. Since I have been visiting the 'taboo loo' I have laughed a great deal and many people have laughed with me. Many more people have come to realise that the loo is really not 'taboo'.

Very simple, but very clear! Photo courtesy of Colin Shakespeare.

Etymological Considerations

Probably the most common name attributed to the privy is 'loo'. This name is in itself an enigma and as such prompts many etymological considerations. Some historians think that 'loo' is derived from the Old English word 'hleow', which means a small shelter. One could consider this quite logical. However, many an old soldier of World War I will tell you that it comes from the observation that the number 100 seemed to be the number on most privy doors in pensions, guesthouses and hotels in France and Belgium at the time and the English soldiers perversely pronounced it 'loo'.

ANOTHER INTERPRETATION COMES from the old French habit of tossing the contents of chamber pots into streets with the shouted warning *'Gardez l'eau!'* The argument runs that a poor English attempt to pronounce the French *'l'eau'* could explain the origin of the term.

In Australia, there is a quaint explanation for the word being used locally. Anything smelly or 'on the nose' was said to be 'down at Woolloomooloo', a somewhat squalid harbourside suburb of Sydney at the time of early settlement. The inference is easy to see.

If an etymologist wanted to research the origins and meanings of names given to the outhouse there is no doubt that he or she would have a lifetime of work guaranteed.

A thatched loo in Berkshire England.

SOME ALTERNATIVES TO PONDER

Abort	German	**Bramah**	English, from J. Bramah, inventor of WC valve, 1778
Ajax	English pun on Jake's Latrine		
Altar Room	USA	**Bumbie**	Southern England
Aunt Mabel	English		
Aunt Mary	English	**Cabinet**	French
Backhouse	USA	**Can**	USA
Big Gulper	USA	**Cannies**	USA and French
Bog	Irish, adopted by the English Army	**Carsey**	English Army, World War I
Bog House	English	**Chamber of Commerce**	USA and English

An abandoned 'bog' in Ring of Kerry, Ireland.

Charlie's Joint	USA	John/Jon	USA
Choo	African	Jones's Place	USA
Closet	English	Kharzi	English Army, from Hindustani
Comfort Wagon	USA		
Convenience	French and English	Klondike	USA
Crapper	English and USA	La La	Australian
		Lavatory	English
Crown Room	English	Little Boy's Room	English
Dagwood's Place	USA	Little House	Universal
Dog House	USA	Midden	English
Donegar	Irish	Morgan's Dyke	West Country England
Down the Back	Universal		
Dub	Australian	Music Room	Australian
Duffs	English schools	Necessary House	English
Dunny	Australian	Netty	Northern Ireland
Dyke	Australian and English		
		Old Henry	USA
Garderobe	English	Old Soldier's Home	English
Gurleroom	USA		
Head	Universal, nautical	Out the Back	English
		Petty	Northern England
Holy of Holies	English and USA		
		Piss House	Universal
Hoosegow	USA	Pissoir	French
House of Commons	English	Poet's Corner	Universal
		Pony	English
House of Lords	English	Powder Room	Universal
House of Parliament	English and Australian	Pride and Joy	Australian and USA
Jake's	English	Privy	Universal
Jerusalem	English Army	Proverbial	Australian

Queen of Sheba	Australian	The You Know Where	Universal	
Reading Room	English			
Rear	USA	Thinking Room	Universal	
Relief Station	USA	Throne Room	Australian and English	
Ruth	USA			
Sanctuary	USA	Thunderbox	Welsh and English Army	
Shiethouse	German origin, universal slang	Toilet	English	
Shouse	Australian, English and USA	Toiletten	European	
		Toot	Australian and English	
Temple	English			
The Observation Room	English and USA	Ty'back	Welsh	
		Water Closet (WC)	Universal	

SOME LIKELY SOURCES

AUNT MARY — Aunties were thought to have excused themselves from the presence of children by saying they were going to a 'special place'. It caught on and became Aunt Mary's Room and then shortened to Aunt Mary.

BOG — When cat-style sanitation was the norm in Ireland people used the peat bog as the convenience.

CRAPPER — Sir Thomas Crapper was instrumental in water closet design. The term 'crap' would have come from this.

DUNEGAN — a privy, a water closet.

DUNNY — from dannaken from danna (dung) + ken (place).

HOUSE OF PARLIAMENT, COMMONS OR LORDS — Perhaps the acts of being seated, presenting papers and then retiring from the house resulted in this term.

NETTY — a Geordie earth closet.

PRIVY — derived from the Latin word 'privatus'.

THUNDERBOX — the privies for underground Welsh miners were specially made boxes located in disused mine shafts. Because of the tunnel acoustics it was said that the miners were making thunder.

LA LA — this could come from the fact that some users sing while in the loo or perhaps it is a child's adaptation of 'lavatory'.

AT CROSS-PURPOSES

MANY A VISITOR has come to grief in a foreign land when not knowing what to ask for when they require the 'necessary house'. The problem is epitomised in a story about a man who came rushing into an outback pub, calling to the barmaid, 'Quick, where's the dunny?' The barmaid, a young English lass on a working holiday, did not know what a dunny was, so in an attempt to hide her ignorance she looked nonchalantly around the shelves believing it was some strange outback drink. When the distressed man said, 'Quick, girl, where is it?' she answered, 'I'll have a look in the refrigerator!'

Another delightful story was sent to me from Adeline Beltzo in the United States. This is one of many variations on this theme.

An English lady, while visiting Switzerland, was looking for a room to let for an extended period so she asked a local schoolmaster

A 'lavatree'! Note the sophisticated corrugated iron roof and the fig tree growing on the right hand side. This will grow very well, fertilised by the pan being emptied onto it! Photo courtesy of Colin Shakespeare.

if he could recommend any. He took her to see several and when everything was settled, the lady returned to her home in England to make final preparations to move. When she arrived home, the thought suddenly occurred to her that she had not seen a WC around the place. She immediately wrote a note to the schoolmaster asking him where the WC was located. The schoolmaster was a poor student of written English, so he asked the local parish priest to help him draft a letter. Together they pondered over the meaning of WC and came to the conclusion that it meant 'Wayside Chapel'. The schoolmaster then sent the following note off to the English lady.

Dear Madam,

I take great pleasure in informing you that the WC is situated nine miles from the house, in the corner of a pine grove. It is capable of seating 220 people and is open on Sundays and Thursdays only. As there are a great number of people expected during the summer months, I would suggest you come early, although there is plenty of standing room. This is an unfortunate situation, particularly if you have a habit of going regularly.

You will no doubt be glad to hear that a good number bring their lunch and make a day of it, while others who can afford to go by car and arrive just in time. I would especially recommend that your ladyship go on Thursday, when there is an organ accompaniment. The acoustics are excellent and even the most delicate sounds can be heard everywhere.

It may interest you to know that my daughter was married in the WC and it was there she first met her husband. I can remember the rush for seats; there were ten people to a seat, usually occupied by one. It was wonderful to see the expressions on their faces.

The newest attraction is a bell donated by a resident of the district. It rings every time a person enters. A bazaar is to be held to provide plush seats for all, since it is a long-felt need by the people. My wife is rather delicate so she can't attend regularly. It is almost a year since she went last. Naturally it pains her very much not to be able to go more often.

I shall be delighted to reserve the best seat for you if you wish, where you will be seen by all. For children there is a special time and place so they will not disturb others.

Sincerely yours ...

Me sitting beside a row of dunnies in Glebe. They are classified by the National Trust. Photo courtesy of the Sydney Morning Herald.

An abandoned and storm-defeated outhouse in the Flinders Ranges, SA.

Looking Back

In 960 AD Etholwold, Abbot of Abingdon in the County of Oxfordshire, is said to have diverted the water from a stream to sanitise the habits of his fellow monks. The leaders of monastic establishments were instrumental in promoting the use of water to cleanse, much to the benefit of the population as a whole.

THE ROMANS HAD also shown enterprise when it came to the use of water. They diverted streams and springs into narrow troughs hewn from rock where up to twenty men could relieve themselves at a time.

Henry III was also keen to pursue the development of sanitation by ordering that 'privies' or 'garderobes' be built in all his houses.

GARDEROBES AND CHAMBER POTS

'GARDEROBE' WAS THE old English name given to the grand chambers that were often buttressed over battlements of houses and castles. These very special places housed a simple hanging arrangement of poles or in some cases formed an integral part of the wall. People sat within these structures and all that fell on the outer side landed in the moat or against the wall, where the waste could be collected, combined with wood ash and used as a fertiliser.

Some garderobes were placed adjacent to the main entrance, whether by design or accident is not known. Perhaps the ploy was to deter visitors! In some situations efforts were made to disguise the outflows using gargoyles at the outlet points. Where outlet points were of large proportions it was necessary to guard them carefully when the castle was under siege. Commanders had no compunction in ordering the lower ranks through the outlet up the garderobe. Another tactic was to seal a skep (hive) of bees into the bottom outlet point of the garderobe and the bees, not being happy about their new location, would infiltrate the castle and add to the misery of the inhabitants.

On occasions garderobes were built alongside chimneys or as an

Just as well we take torches everywhere we go! My son and I are checking out a garderobe outlet (no longer in use!) at Harlech Castle, Wales. The castle was built in 1283 by Edward I.

integral part of the chimney, not only for warmth but to assist with the disposal of odours; the outlet arrangement could also be disguised as a chimneysweep hole.

Dwellings that did not have the luxury of a garderobe on the higher floors required the inhabitants or guests to refrain from using the fireplace as a privy. Ashes in the fireplace would disguise their activities for a time but eventually the consequences of their actions caught up with them and resulted in severe reprimands. It is difficult to imagine a host suggesting to a casual occupant of a room without a garderobe but with a fireplace, 'If you please, do not use the fireplace as a loo during your stay.'

Here is another garderobe outlet, in Ireland this time. The outlet is on the left corner, third floor. Just as well it's not directly above the front door! The different textures of stone are probably the result of repairs after the building was attacked.

Jonathan Swift, who was a dab hand at penning the odd privy ditty, wrote a directive in 1745 aimed at servant ladies of the period who thought the comforts of a 'joynte-stoole' (chamber pot) preferable to facing the elements of the backyard:

> I am very offended with those ladies, who are so proud and lazy, they will not be at pains at stepping out into the garden to 'pluck a rose', but keep an odious implement sometimes in the bed chamber itself or at least in the dark closet adjoining, which they make use of to ease their worsest necessities, and you are the usual carriers away of the pan, which maketh not only the chamber but the clothes offensive to all who come near. Now, to cure them of this odious practice, let me advise you on whom this office lieth, to convey away this utensil, that you will do it openly down the great stairs, and in the presence of the footman; and if anybody knocketh, to open.

Outside on the streets and surrounds, conditions were even worse. The streets of London in the 1300s were far from sanitary. A royal writ commanding the Chancellor of London University to clean up the streets was issued in 1358. It was no wonder, when nearly every outlet to the River Thames was knee deep in filth.

These were the days when the contents of chamber pots were thrown out windows, often landing on the unwary. Pedestrians on their everyday business kept as near as possible to the centre of passageways and away from overhanging houses. In Paris this practice continued until a wealthy Parisian marquis received the entire contents of a chamber pot, which ruined not only his new *paletot* (loose cloak) but also his appointment with a lady. As a consequence, the practice of emptying pots into the street in Paris was forbidden in 1395.

A very old lavatory in Selby, Yorkshire, England. These were usually in the cloisters of monasteries. The drawing is from Classic Dictionary of Architecture, *by J. Henry Parker, 1846.*

Unbelievably it took until 1750 before the same law was applied to the cities and towns of Britain. Progress demanded that something be done, so the invention of the simple wooden commode was popularly acclaimed. This, however, did not eliminate the problem of waste disposal. Sewerage systems were still a long way off and it was not until 1843 in Britain that reticulated sewerage systems were introduced. Wastes therefore had to be collected and disposed of — enter the sanno-man!

GONGFERMORS AND SEWER SAILORS

THE FIRST SANNO-MEN were called 'gongfermors' (from the Saxon *'gong'*, to go, and *'fey'*, to cleanse). They were employed to remove privy contents in the cities. These strangely garbed characters would flit from house to house with two wooden tubs suspended from their shoulders by a simple wooden yoke. As a means of protecting the public, both shoulders and buckets were covered with a cloak. A macabre sight indeed! Gongfermors employed apprentices, usually boys, whose unpleasant task it was to rake the load and handle the horse. The contents of the cart were thrown into the Thames.

Although gongferming was an unsavoury task, it was sought after in times when having a paid job was all that one could wish for. Gongfermors, like their descendants the sanitary men of the twentieth century, became social outcasts mainly due to the aura of the trade that surrounded them.

When underground sewerage pipes were installed the equivalent of gongfermors worked by underground candlelight in search of coins, fragments of metals and other saleable items that managed to slip down the loo. There are men who still work the sewers in the large cities of the world. In Sydney they are called 'sewer sailors' and are employed by the Water Board. These people travel around in two-man canoes in the sewers, armed only with a paddle and a torch. They are not searching for valuables but are inspecting the system for malfunctions and flaws.

'Inspector of Nuisance' (cartoon by Will Pearce).

The sewerage system carries industrial and household effluent to the ocean. In a story by Lydia Roberts for the *Sydney Morning Herald's Good Weekend* about the activities in the tunnels, drains and sewer systems of Sydney and Melbourne, she quotes the project officer as describing the smell as 'just a bit like a bad drain. Mind you, after falling in you wouldn't want to bite your fingernails.'

The longest journey for the Sydney sewer sailors, or 'drain brains', is from Balmain to Bondi, usually a day trip with a lunch break somewhere beneath the Central Business District. At the end of the journey the men scrub themselves with disinfectant but, says the project officer, ' the board used to lay on saunas for the crew after each sail to get the dirt from every nook and cranny'.

WATER CLOSETS AND INSPECTORS OF NUISANCE

IN EARLIER DAYS on the streets of London and other cities of the world, public facilities were almost non-existent except for the public urine stations. Pots were placed at busy intersection points so passers-by could use them. These stations were established not because the authorities were pursuing a 'clean city' policy but because urine was used by leather traders, dye manufacturers and laundry owners. The laundry owners, for example, used urine to make lye for the bleaching of bed linen. These public urine stations were eventually outlawed in the interests of public health and, to enforce the law, 'Inspectors of Nuisance' were appointed.

The introduction of the British Public Health Act in 1848 was the first serious attempt to clean up London. In fact this Act probably set the standards for modern-day health Acts throughout the

Two sceptical-looking 'sewer sailors'. Photo courtesy the NSW Water Board.

English-speaking world, as did the Building Acts written as a consequence of the Fire of London in 1666.

Physician and social reformer Sir Edwin Chadwick (1800–90) was instrumental in 'cleaning up the closets', but it wasn't until 1875 that it was compulsory for every house to have a proper earth, ash or water closet. Water closets were an improvement on the earth and ash closets, but not all people could afford to install them. Thus began the journey 'down the back'. Interior earth and ash closets were not totally acceptable due to odour, so many an outhouse was built away from the house.

Queen Ann introduced one of the first water closets at Windsor Castle in 1710. In 1755 Alex Cummings patented the commercial WC. However, long before the installation of Queen Ann's WC primitive forms of water closets were being experimented with. The Elizabethan poet, John Harington, designed one and had it installed in his country home near Bath in 1589. A local artisan was employed to do the job as Sir John wasn't too nifty with plumbing or carpentry tools. Unfortunately the artisan is only known by his initials, T.C.

Many early water closets were ornately decorated, depicting floral arrangements and country landscapes. I understand that HRH Prince Charles has a collection of decorated pedestals.

On the streets, public toilets were going up-market. By the mid-1850s public toilets containing water closets were being installed. The first was a Gents opened at 95 Fleet Street by the Society of Arts on 2 February 1852. One for ladies, situated in Bedford Street near the Strand, was opened nine days later. These facilities were intended for the benefit of the middle classes as the costs to enter were relatively high: twopence for the use of the basic amenity and another twopence for washing of hands, brushes and clothes. The not-so-rich had a choice of either not venturing too far from home or visiting the common privy — not such a pleasant experience!

THE LOCAL SCENE

IN AUSTRALIA, technology meant the upgrading of our facilities as well. Bush folk were keeping to their old ways but city dwellers had to be regulated. Prior to the mid-1850s the cities were in utter chaos with respect to sanitation. Acute health problems forced government intervention. Initially, some well-intentioned official efforts were of questionable value. In 1855, for example, the Commissioners of the City of Sydney reported that the government had given permission for councils' night soil to be 'deposited in the sandhills along Coogee Road'. Unfortunately, the site drained into Busby's Bore, the main source of Sydney's water supply at the time.

THE SEPTIC SCENE

EVENTUALLY SEWERAGE RETICULATION SYSTEMS reached out to many cities and villages all over the world. For those not within reach of this new technology, the safe and efficient septic system was being recommended by the modern-day 'Nuisance Inspector'. Little houses at the bottom of the yard were being converted; pan and pit loos were becoming endangered species.

Septic tanks work on the principle of anaerobic bacterial action and discharge clean water. When the use of septic tanks was being encouraged, one advocate actually drank a glass of the discharge water to prove the system's effectiveness. The safe and hygienic septic system was available to all, provided there was an adequate water supply to keep the system going.

COMING IN FROM THE COLD

THE NEW HYGIENIC SYSTEMS meant that the privy could be moved inside. However, many folk found it hard to accept change and, initially, moving the loo inside was unacceptable. In addition, they couldn't adjust to the idea of not being able to continue the lifelong ritual of 'going down the back'. As a result many flush toilets were simply connected to the old faithful and life went on as normal.

With the entry of the flush toilet into the house and the new popularity enjoyed by barbecues an old timer observed, 'I can't understand them these days. In my day we ate inside and went to the dunny outside. Nowadays they eat outside and go to the dunny inside!'

In the back lanes of Broken Hill, NSW. Note how the can-access hole has been filled in.

Sanno-men
and
Flaming
Furies

Having a loo at the bottom of the garden was not without its problems, because wastes still had to be disposed of. With the growth of communities local authorities were forced to take on the responsibility of waste disposal. For houses not connected to a sewerage system the service provided was technically known as the 'night collection service', and even though it was an unpleasant job it was sought after because it paid well.

RESIDENTS WITHOUT A council collection service had to take things into their own hands. The task was usually bestowed on the man of the house, who armed himself with a spade and then endeavoured to select a spot not previously dug. This unpopular means of disposal did, however, have advantages. If the householders were intent on winning flower and vegetable competitions at local agricultural shows, they certainly knew where to plant the seedlings.

Because there were problems from a space and effort point of view with the digging of holes in one's backyard, some people used their neighbours' loos. One lady, whose chore it was to dig a hole in her backyard because she lived too far away for the council night service, came to the conclusion that her can seemed to be filling far too often so she secretly numbered the toilet paper sheets. It was as she thought: the neighbour and her brood were taking advantage of her can instead of using their own. Her husband devised a plan and the next evening when shadows appeared, he struck. Removing the rear hatch he poked in a bunch of stinging nettles. Out shot a rather gargantuan lady, who was never to trespass again!

With the introduction of the night collection service the sanno-man came to the fore. The men who took on this vital task (there are no records yet turned up to indicate that a woman was ever employed as a sanno-carter) acquired various names such as san-man, sanno-man, wanderer of the night, whoopee steward, bumbie man, honey man, nightman and nightsoil man.

Few householders ever met their sanno-man, as he was required by law to do his duty during the wee small hours. Only those householders who frequented the loo late at night or those who rose early would encounter him. One lady who rose early was sitting comfortably when the sanno-man arrived. He opened the access door at the back, whipped out the can from under her and called, 'Thanks, luv!'

One thoughtful sanitary carter attached a bell to his cart so occupants of the loo could hear him coming. Rather than be embarrassed, they could vacate the loo when they heard the bell. This sanno cart was known as the 'Hum Dinger'.

For those without a back lane access the sanno-man had to enter through the front gate and proceed down the side passage. This route had the potential to cause the sanno-man and the householder some distress if there were any obstacles in the way over which the sanno-man might trip. On the afternoon prior to the nightman's visit it was 'all hands on deck' to clear the route. Toys, garden tools, hoses and bikes all had to be moved out of the way and if the nightman's technique was to carry the can on his shoulder then it was imperative that the clothesline was up well above shoulder height.

Again it's the festive season,
And the end of year is nigh,
So we have every reason
To heave a heavy sigh.
It's the last year of our contract,
And soon we'll down our load;
No more along your garden track
We'll stagger to the road.
We wish you a happy Christmas,
With loads of fun and cheer,
We've served you very faithfully,
Throughout the dying year.
If you have a little something,
To help our Christmas treat,
We thank you very kindly —
Just leave it on the seat.

THE SAN-MEN

Here is the artistic and poetic Christmas message left for householders by the sanno-men in Mt Isa, Qld. Hope it did the trick!

Regardless of precautions, sanno-men did have accidents. There are records of a sanno-man falling into a swimming pool, and others, having partaken of too much Christmas cheer, have had indescribable disasters. One such adventure befell Bill, whose sanno cart had tipped over. A passerby remarked, 'Bad luck Bill, you've had an accident.' Bill replied, 'No, I'm just stocktaking.'

There are many similar stories worldwide relating to the sanno-men. Among the more pleasant are those surrounding Christmas. Each year at this time some turned to prose to express their feelings of goodwill and to drum up some offerings from those they had serviced throughout the year. A bottle of beer, some cigarettes or even a handkerchief and socks would lighten the sanno-man's load in the coming year. A little gift guaranteed no slip-ups in the backyard. The verse, sometimes poorly written, was at least enter-taining and these poetic Christmas cards were left on the privy seat.

PLUMBING THE DEPTHS

NOT ALL HOUSEHOLDERS were in need of the sanno-man's services. Those who had a cesspit-style outhouse had to attend to their own affairs, and their problems were similar to those of centuries before. Stories abound about the problems of pit-style loos. Many an animal or family pet has fallen down the pit and become trapped. Imagine being comfortably seated when a voice from down below calls, 'Scratch cocky!' This happened some years back when one pet cockatoo fell down the pit, unbeknownst to its owners.

Retrieving animals, and even children, from a pit required ingenuity and forward planning. Snakes in pits caused much consternation. Usually all work stopped around workplaces such as

Pro Hart is probably the only Australian painter who has painted the actual moving of a loo from one hole to another. This painting, like many of his other works, depicts the ordinary lives of bush folk from a past era. It is set in the barren but colourful district of Broken Hill, NSW.

woolsheds until the snake was removed. A shotgun blast down a pit to dispatch a snake was not recommended, as this caused Newton's Laws of Motion to come into play: reaction is always equal and opposite to action. One shearing shed organiser whose job it was to ensure conditions around the woolshed were to the liking of the shearers found this out when he tried to dispatch a snake from a multi-holer dunny!

For pure inventiveness a story related by Peg Shapcott of Coonabarabran in New South Wales takes the cake:

> When our daughter was young her kitten fell down the loo.
> We were out and she couldn't wait for us to come home to
> help her as Kitty was meowing frantically and she was beside

herself. What was she to do? She remembered a story she had
read where a cat had been retrieved from a well using a
bucket tied to a piece of rope, so she tied a billy can to a string
and as an incentive for Kitty to get into the billy she put a
piece of meat in the bottom. After several unsuccessful
attempts she finally managed to get Kitty out. The cleaning of
Kitty is another story!

People who carried items on their belts in days gone by can relate
stories of how a valuable item became disconnected and fell down
the pit. Tobacco, penknives and money pouches have fallen to the
depths and because they were valuable the owners had no
alternative but to retrieve them. One gent lost a gold sovereign
down a pit and while attempting to 'fish' it out was uttering a few
vulgarisms. A neighbour, hearing his distress, called, 'Why don't
you throw a few more in and make it worth your while?'

Problems with younger children occurred if the older children
managed to convince a sibling that hell existed down the pit. It was
then very difficult to persuade the younger ones to go to the
outhouse unaccompanied.

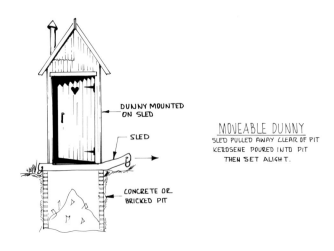

DUNNY MOUNTED ON SLED

SLED

MOVEABLE DUNNY
SLED PULLED AWAY CLEAR OF PIT
KEROSENE POURED INTO PIT
THEN SET ALIGHT.

CONCRETE OR BRICKED PIT

Another problem with pits occurred when the hole reached capacity and the structure over the pit had to be moved to a new site, which entailed a lot of work. The actual moving operation often turned into a social event, with neighbours coming to lend a hand. One way of overcoming this chore was to dig a large pit and build a multi-holer structure, which meant that one could move from hole to hole allowing the full section to settle over a period of time.

One innovative dunny builder decided to overcome the problem of filling pits by building a standard-size single hole loo over an extra large pit. Sheets of corrugated iron were placed over the parts of the pit not covered by the dunny. Earth was then placed over the iron to tidy up the whole affair. Over the years grass grew over the iron and eventually the iron rusted leaving a very unstable surface around the dunny. Fortunately, when the dunny surrounds inevitably collapsed, it was a pet lamb that had the misfortune to fall through into the pit, and not a human visitor. However, as Kathleen Stewart of Murrurundi tells the story, it was a far from pleasant task for her mother to retrieve and clean up the lamb.

When cameras became the norm children would insist that Dad take their photograph standing in the new hole. (A frustrating aspect for the privyologist is that few photographs exist of very old outhouses. It seems it was not the done thing to photograph the loo.)

FLAMING FURIES

COMBUSTIBLE LOOS WERE an alternative way of dealing with full holes. In northern parts of Australia combustibles pouting chimney-style flue pipes were known as 'flaming furies'. Kerosene or distillate was poured into the pit and set alight. Fortunately, in the towns where combustible toilets were in vogue most townsfolk agreed to light up on the same day, thus reducing prolonged periods of atmospheric pollution.

Outhouses that were not specifically designed for burning off rarely caught fire, but when fire was introduced there were some disastrous consequences. If care was not taken when flushing out a red-back spider with a lighted taper, a spark could fall into the pit and set fire to the paper down below, resulting in an unintentional flaming fury. Another cause of accidental burning was lighted cigarette butts being disposed of down the pit, the culprits often being youngsters interrupted when taking the forbidden puff. In these cases the privy would not burn down immediately as paper in the pit would only smoulder and then burst into flames later.

Fire has often been used in latrines, especially during war time. Many a soldier has had tricks played on him when making a visit to the communal loo. One system of latrine entailed the erection of seats over a running stream. For a joke a lighted piece of paper could be dropped in upstream and it would float down, giving an

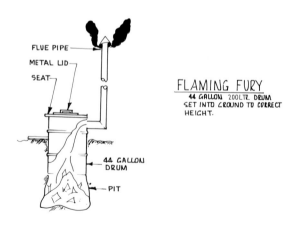

FLAMING FURY
44 GALLON 200LTR. DRUM
SET INTO GROUND TO CORRECT HEIGHT.

unusually warming feeling to the visitor. Another war-time joke was played on one sergeant major in the habit of having a cigarette in the latrine and throwing his match into the pit. The non-commissioned ranks extracted cordite (an explosive substance used in munitions) and placed it in the pit. The resultant explosion when the match was dropped provided much entertainment for the practical jokers, but left the sergeant major far from amused.

A Flaming Fury (cartoon by Will Pearce).

Techniques of Building and Privies with Class

Prior to government regulations just about anyone considered they were adequately qualified to build a privy. Outhouses built before regulations came in place were mostly jerry built, but occasionally a professional was called in. These dedicated craftsmen knew the importance of location and the benefits of selecting the sight for the best view. Having an outhouse face east meant that the user could do a spot of early morning sunbathing. Doors on such privies had to swing in so that if someone was heard approaching the door could be kicked shut.

LOCATION IS EVERYTHING

ALL OVER THE WORLD outhouses have been located for the best view. Down the garden path, as they say in Britain, at Poppet Sands Youth Hostel there is a tremendous view from a disused privy, looking down the Teif River estuary. Others that take in the views of England's rolling hills and moors and the highlands of Scotland leave one with a certain appreciation for nature.

Views from outhouses in Australia vary due to the diverse topography. However, the most impressive are to be found in the outback around the Flinders Ranges, on the edge of the Great Victorian Desert and on the Nullarbor Plain. These dunnies of the latter are the most isolated and must have the widest vista of any in Australia, and possibly the world.

The Nullarbor Plain dunnies are not the only ones standing in total isolation. There are many scattered throughout the Australian countryside standing silently aloof. One might ask why. One explanation might be that the original house to which the loo belonged had burnt down, and because the dunny stood some distance from the house it did not suffer the same fate. The dunny thus survived to become one of the great icons of the Australian countryside.

On the opal fields, outhouses of all shapes and sizes are perched atop disused mine shafts. Mullock heaps extend for as far as the eye can see. Because of soaring summer temperatures miners and their families live underground. The only above-ground activity that the visitor to these isolated communities might see may be the underground dwellers emerging to satisfy their calls of nature.

On the Abrolhos Islands off the coast of Western Australia improvisation has come to the fore once more in creating an

A loo loo of a view!
But there can be
problems — the lady
of the house was once
sitting, admiring the
view, when a head
appeared over the cliff
edge, peering at her!

unusual vista of outhouses perched above high tide level at the end of rickety piers. These loos are true water closets and there are no problems with waste disposal, as fish abound.

A toilet facility perched over water is no modern-day innovation. As far back as the twelfth century public privies were incorporated into London Bridge. These loos were used for two hundred years before rotting timbers could no longer take the load and the whole affair, including the occupants at the time, fell into the River Thames. As was said at that time: 'Wise men went across the bridge and fools went under.'

ENGINEERING FEATS

MATERIALS USED FOR building outhouses varied: stone, brick, weatherboard, rough-sawn timber, corrugated iron and flattened oil drums have all been used, and pan services have even been set up in the hollows of trees. Some privies were built into stone and brick walls because fewer materials were needed and the structure acted as a buttress which strengthened the wall.

Here is a Welsh 'thunder box'. It is built into the stone wall. They used huge corner stones (quoins), and pieces of slate for the stepping stones. This was a very cold and bleak spot for a visit to the loo!

Many outhouses had low roofs, often just high enough to stand up in. Structures came in all shapes and sizes — they might have flat, barrel-vaulted (self-supporting) or gable roofs. Some were attached to farm buildings and houses and some even had dovecotes in their roofs. One Queensland outhouse was constructed with a pole frame. Four poles were sunk into the ground and boards were nailed horizontally to the poles — but only halfway up! The builder apparently ran out of boards midway through construction and the structure stayed half clad for nearly twenty years.

Here is another abandoned loo attracting junk in the central west of NSW.

HOME IMPROVEMENTS AND EXTENSIONS

OUTHOUSES OFTEN BECAME a collecting point for junk, a function that led to the creation of adjoining structures. The most common addition was a wood shed. Having the wood shed by the dunny meant that people returning to the house could bring a piece of wood back with them. Having a heap in this location also provided an opportunity for the shy ladies of the house to excuse themselves without actually going into explicit detail; 'I'm going to get a piece of wood,' they would say. If they were unsure whether the little house was occupied they could 'fiddle' around the wood heap discreetly before entering. A number of false runs throughout the day would mean a full wood box.

ADAPTATIONS AND REINCARNATIONS

ABANDONED OUTHOUSES ARE now used for purposes other than those for which they were originally intended. Bush folk, being masters of recycling, have converted disused loos into dog kennels, tool sheds and pump houses. One enterprising owner even converted a dunny to a barbecue. However, the prize for lateral thinking must go to the lady who had her outhouse converted into a bin for the storing of recyclable plastic milk bottles. The door was modified so that the empty bottles could be thrown over the top.

The Wongarbon Railway outhouse, in NSW, on its way to total demolition.

Classified

The significance of the outhouse as part of our national heritage is at last being officially recognised. A number of semi-government organisations have acknowledged that the dunny in isolation or included with other buildings should be preserved. One example is a vintage (1803) nine-holer at Hobartville near Richmond, New South Wales. This classic privy was possibly designed by noted colonial architect Francis Greenway (1777–1837).

ANOTHER CLASSIC MULTI-HOLER is at Denham Court west of Sydney; it is believed to have been built in the 1830s. It consists of a two-room timber building about six metres long and three metres wide. Each room has a bench with two holes which open into a pit. An old and well-nourished bougainvillea covers the back of the building.

Recognition of the heritage value of the 'little house' we knew so well has not come soon enough. Many have been destroyed. An example is the Wongarbon railway outhouse (circa 1880). Wongarbon is a small village near Dubbo, in western New South Wales. Locals used to brag about their icon with its chimney. The brick outhouse had a permanent pit sanitary system, a very common facility when it was not feasible to move the building to a new hole. When the pit was filled up it had to be dug out, access being via a trapdoor at the back. Usually an inmate from the local police cells carried out this task.

The Wongarbon outhouse was a striking piece with its chimney and one could be forgiven for thinking that it could have been a combustible type, but this was not the case. Research into State Rail Authority archives revealed that the original plan had no provisions for a chimney. However, upon further investigation it was found that the master bricklayer thought it a good idea to give apprentices practice at building chimneys — erecting one on a dunny seemed as good a place as any to start.

The Wongarbon outhouse fell into disuse and was converted firstly into a milking bail and then into a pig sty. For no apparent reason it was eventually demolished — it was not until then the locals and users of the highway nearby realised what they had lost. But we live and learn and maybe next time, when an endangered species is threatened, those responsible for cleaning up the landscape will think twice.

Across the Atlantic in the United States the 'backhouse' has also received rightful recognition. Two of the more famous, now restored and classified, are those designed by America's third president, Thomas Jefferson. Jefferson longed for the solitude of a hermit so he designed and had built a hide-away near Lynchburg, Virginia in 1806. Along with other majestic buildings, two privies were built which he called 'cloacinas'. They were octagonal in shape and hidden from view by twin circular grassy mounds topped with weeping willows.

Jefferson's 'cloacina'. Photo courtesy of The Corporation for Jefferson's Poplar Forest.

The multi-holer at Shadforth Public School, in NSW.

Fine Details, Seats and Lids

Many out-of-town outhouses had the seating arrangements constructed on the spot and in many respects were primitive in the extreme. However, there were some basic principles. For example, any good carpenter knew that a proper hole needed a point at the front and that setting out was important.

IF THE SEAT was made from one slab of timber, the piece cut out could be used as a bread board. If the seat was made to accommodate workers the idea was not to make the seat too smooth, otherwise the workers might stay longer than necessary. The actual size of the hole depended of course on the size of the user. It stood to reason that for children, smaller-sized holes were required otherwise they could slip and become stuck. Relaxation was usually the reason for slipping.

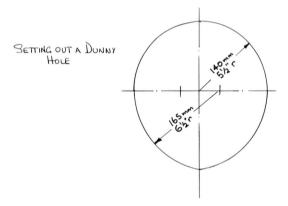

SETTING OUT A DUNNY HOLE

SLIPPAGE

SOMETIMES COMPLETE RELAXATION could lead to sleep. Many a worker would 'nip off' to the loo for a breather. An ingenious seat design to eliminate the chances of a worker 'nodding off' was a seat sloping forward, which meant excessive relaxation resulted in the user falling off and therefore waking up. This innovation originated in Port Kembla, New South Wales. There, around the coke ovens, high levels of the deadly gas carbon monoxide could lead to loo users falling asleep and never waking up. With a sloping seat they would be rudely awakened.

GREAT WESTERN RLY
NOTICE
WORKMEN'S LAVATORY

WORKMEN USING THIS CLOSET MUST ON ENTERING GIVE THEIR TICKET NUMBERS TO THE ATTENDANT. IF LONGER TIME THAN TEN MINUTES IS TAKEN THE WHOLE TIME WILL BE STOPPED.

APRIL 1904   **BY ORDER**

Above: Dunny designers needed to ensure workers did not stay in their facilities longer than absolutely necessary.

A hollow stump, plank seat combination — primitive in the extreme! Note the cypress pine roof. Also note the rotten corn sack 'door' and the nails (ow!) sticking up through the seat.

MATERIALS

SEATS WERE NOT always made of wood; many were made from whatever was at hand. Around Festiniog in northern Wales and Mintaro in South Australia, both slate-producing areas, seats were made of slate — long-lasting, but a little cold on a frosty morning. Today seats that are thermostatically warmed can be bought by those who are sensitive to the cold — a far cry from the rough old seats of yesteryear.

Bench seats made from crude wooden boards had disadvantages, especially if the boards worked loose. The loose boards could give the users a nasty nip if they rocked about or did not rise squarely.

People of means had a choice of purchasing hand-carved seats made from solid oak, cherry wood, maple or cedar. In fact the sales pitch would be: 'made to your size'. Dressing up the closet became big business. Trade catalogues were aimed mainly at the lady of the house because she was usually responsible for keeping the outhouse clean, scrubbing the seat with sand soap or lemon juice.

AUTOMATIC DISINFECTING TANK

STEEL P.V.C. COATED SEAT

WEBSTER SUPERB
DRAWING ADAPTED FROM LINE DRAWING
FROM WEBSTER CATALOGUE.

Here we have the patented disinfectant accessory for the pan loo. The reservoir would be filled with disinfectant, which would drip out through the cone outlet on the bottom. The board seat looks a bit rough and cracked too — not very appealing, judging from the look on young Tim's face!

Catalogues were beautifully illustrated with line drawings to emphasise a sales point.

Eventually, wooden seats became unfashionable and were replaced by some novel alternatives. One such innovation was a specially designed lid to which was attached a small tank filled with disinfectant; when the lid was closed a squirt of disinfectant dropped into the pan. A celebrated line of sanitary closets fitted with such a device was the Webster Superb. It was marketed aggressively with the slogan: 'No flies on Webster'. The Webster Superb boasted a virtually indestructible lid made from steel and coated with plastic. The distributor, Charles Savage, demonstrated his lid at the Royal Easter Agricultural Show in Sydney in the 1950s. Charlie would make a point by attacking the seat with an axe to demonstrate the seat's indestructibility. Some visitors to the show remember his antics well and he was widely regarded as 'the highlight of the show'.

Advancements in plastic injection-moulding techniques have meant that the plastic seat is now the norm. When the new-fangled plastic seats became readily available some folk simply attached the plastic seat to the top of the bench seat. An example of this was seen in a public toilet at a recreational reserve in Sheffield, Tasmania. A cheap plastic seat was nailed on to a wooden seat using galvanised roofing nails — not just one but near a dozen, all coming into contact with bare flesh. Sleeping on a bed of nails had nothing on the Sheffield dunny.

INNOVATIONS

SEATS AND LIDS are the areas in which engineers and inventors have experimented most. Maybe they are inspired to improve things while in the 'thinking room'. On average, an Australian can spend up to five thousand hours in the loo in a lifetime. It's no wonder that it is called the thinking room.

One thinker came up with a combined seat and lid contraption that incorporated two steel flaps which opened when the users sat down. The moment they stood up, two springs brought the flaps back to the horizontal position rather sharply. One can imagine the consequences if the mechanics failed. Gertrude Skinner of Tamworth remembers this model well because of a visit to a cousin in Gunnedah, and she penned the following verses:

The Funny Dunny

My cousin had this dunny
At her home in Gunnedah
Two parts, there were to its lid
And made to come ajar.

Because I was unsure of it,
I squatted right on top,
So I could look upon its lid,
And watch my droppings drop.

I know you won't believe it,
A crack came open wide,
And down fell my contributions
To the dark depths, there inside.

And as I slid down off it,
The crack began to close,
While I stood there in wonderment,
And mumbled 'Stone the crows!'

Marie Hombsch of Tamworth and her toddler son encountered a 'Funny dunny' thirty-five years ago at a holiday house at Port Macquarie, New South Wales.

The toilet was under the tank stand. It was lined with Malthoid, a black tar-impregnated paper, so the area was dark and airless. I had never seen the like.

To use the toilet you lifted the lid to find another lid — this proved to be two downward-opening flaps forced open by your own body weight when you sat down. Oh the joy of continuing the toilet training of our small son, when his body weight was not sufficient to open the flaps. Can you imagine

Another golden oldie! The box for small people's feet is a thoughtful touch, isn't it? It adds that something extra to a solid and practical, but not very user-friendly loo.

holding a child with both hands, standing on one leg trying to apply the right amount of pressure to the right spot in order to open the flaps. The child was terrified. We both came away crying, and covered with sweat as it was as 'hot as hell' in there. It didn't take long for commonsense to prevail, and to solve the problem we went to a secluded area near the chookyard to 'kill the ants'.

The best part of that holiday was returning home to our farm, with its lovely, sunny, flushing septic system.

Then there were the multi-holers. Seats with several holes had special uses. First, children obviously needed smaller holes or else they could slip through and become stuck. A small hole and a large hole next to each other also simplified toilet training. Once the little folk had gained confidence and ventured down the back alone a cow bell placed on the seat was an ideal way to summon Mum, although many would just call incessantly, 'I'm finished!' In days gone by, it was generally agreed that when children progressed to the big hole they had at last grown up.

FROG HOLES

MENTION MUST BE MADE, however, of loos without seats. Many visitors to Asia, the Mediterranean or the Middle East have tales of encounters with this style of privy. The problem for those used to the pedestal is that complete relaxation is not possible — it is a business only visit. Squat, or 'frog holes' as they are affectionately known, consist of an elongated hole in the floor sometimes with foot plates so that accurate alignment can be achieved. Those not accustomed to this system sometimes find a trip to the toilet far from pleasurable. By the same token those not familiar with the pedestal loo have just as much trouble coming to grips with the Western form. Adaptation is simply a matter of overcoming cultural inheritance.

A beautiful nine-holer at 'Hobartville', Richmond, NSW.

A wooden latch made from the arm of an old chair — nothing wasted in the bush!

Doors and Fittings

By now the reader will know that from a comfort point of view, doors should swing inwards. For practicality, however, they should swing outwards. There have been cases where people have taken ill in the outhouse, fallen forward and become jammed against the door. If the door swings inward, rescuers have to remove the door or go in via a window to gain access.

HANGING A DOOR might seem a straightforward and simple task but, as with most things, forward planning is required. If one likes to admire the view while in the loo, having the door swing open is a distinct advantage. If the door was in the habit of not swinging the way one wanted, a house brick, a cast-iron foot from an old bath or a heavy Mother Potts's iron would suffice to keep the door in the required position.

When dunnies were converted to pedestal loos sometimes the old faithful's physical dimensions were not large enough to accommodate the new technology, especially if the door swung inwards. The odd outhouse has been found with the pedestal profile cut out of the door to allow the door to clear the pedestal.

Around the turn of the century, many factory loos did not have doors. This allowed the foremen to inspect the booths for malingerers — ideal for production bosses but not for workers if they were on serious and genuine business. This outlandish regulation was abandoned following union pressure, but even then half doors were installed that allowed the bosses to peep under the doors to see if the booths were occupied.

Sometimes a trip to the outhouse could be quite an expedition because it was located at such a distance from the house. It was frustrating to make a trip down the back to find someone in occupancy. A number of methods were devised so that intending users of the loo could see if it was occupied from a distance. A crude but effective system comprised of a string attached to the top of the door which passed through a pulley mounted on top of the privacy screen. On the end of the string was a beer bottle. When the door was shut (occupied) the bottle would be at ground level. When the door was open (vacant) the bottle was further up the screen.

Outhouse doors provided an opportunity for creative talent and innovation. On full length doors it was customary to cut the top of the door in a sawtooth pattern, which provided ventilation. Other forms of ventilation were by way of holes cut in the door itself. A twin heart profile signified newlyweds while a bunch of grapes indicated that the owners were well heeled (there was a higher labour content involved with cutting this shape) although simple shapes such as diamonds and crescent moons were most common. One owner when questioned on why his dunny door had only one heart said that the door was not the original and that the first door had had twin hearts. He explained that the new design was adopted because 'Mum and I have been married for so long we have become one.'

Here are some very fancy, and expensive-looking toilets indeed — in a plumbing store in Tabuk, Saudi Arabia. Some even have gold leaf on them! Not necessarily typical of what you would see throughout that country, though. Photo courtesy of Bob Thompson.

Often the environment dictated door design. One example was on an outhouse at Mt Bogong in Victoria. To take advantage of the wonderful alpine view, the owners fitted a stable door. The top section could be kept open, permitting appreciation of the view, and the bottom section could be closed for privacy! This outhouse was claimed to be at the highest altitude in Australia.

In remote parts of Australia many dunnies had no doors at all; there was simply no need. Others may have had a corn or potato sacking, but these materials didn't last long because the sacking deteriorated quickly in exposed conditions. Such doors were no good for hanging coats on so hooks had to be provided on side walls. As mentioned previously, anyone could build a dunny but only the expert, the specialist privyologist, knew the fine tricks of the trade such as knowing where and how high to put a coat hook. Even today, coat hooks not placed above eye height can be dangerous. Many eyes have been poked on hooks not set at a correct height.

Another way to close the door. This one uses a hasp and a staple, wth a stick. There is an old tap washer under the nail, too. Whatever works!

Door catches were made from a variety of materials and the designs varied considerably. The most common design was the Suffolk thumb latch, but on a more primitive level a piece of wire, string or, probably the most common, a little strap of leather that was hooked on a nail would suffice.

People can really improvise with style sometimes! This is a simple but effective latch which uses nothing more exotic than wood, corrugated iron, nuts and bolts and an old handle.

Reading Matter and Other Paper

Few outhouses had a bookshelf. Some perhaps had the odd magazine on the bench seat but no serious provision was made for the bookworm as old-style outhouses were not the best places in which to linger. Since the introduction of the less odorous water closet people have found it quite pleasant to stay a little longer and now some modern loos have books on hand.

O NE MODERN-DAY ENTHUSIAST not content with dressing up the exterior of his loo has a bookshelf with encyclopaedias, an English–Latin dictionary, an atlas, penholder with pad for jotting down inspirations, an incense burner and dunny memorabilia. The peace and quiet of this outhouse with library accords with the euphemism 'the reading room'. Sometimes this particular enthusiast takes a portable telephone with him when conducting important business of the day, which includes telephoning his mother. 'Mum doesn't mind where I ring from as long as I ring.'

Another enthusiast's loo. This one has a bookshelf, speakers, a beautiful toilet-roll holder, squares of newspaper, and a visitors' book on the seat, not to mention the ceramic loo reproductions on the top shelf. It happens to be made out of 100-year-old cypress pine, too. As a final touch, when you sit on the seat — music plays!

THE PAPER CHASE

WHAT IS READ in the reading room? Certainly not Latin poems nowadays, although at one time they were. Lord Chesterfield (the British statesman and wit) recalled in 1747 that he knew a man who always read Latin poems in the necessary house. He also used the poems he read after each sitting for the 'said purpose', steadily working his way through book after book. In much the same style but on a lower intellectual level, people all over the world made good use of old telephone books, trade catalogues and, if they had influence with the local 'fruito', tissue from around apples and pears, which was most suitable. Some users of 'fruito' tissue would iron it flat and smooth before cutting it into squares.

Newspaper squares were probably the most common. The disadvantage of newspaper squares was the frustration the sitters experienced if they were inclined to read the squares and they found that the next square of the article was missing. Many people remember that as children they were employed to tear large format newspapers into useable-sized squares and thread them on to a string. One lady stated, 'As a child I would never include a piece of paper with a face on it because the face might see me when I used it.' Another said, 'I would go through all the squares and find the face I didn't like and use that one.' In a small country town years ago the father of the bride would not allow his daughter's wedding photograph to be published in the local paper. 'I'm not having my daughter's face being used in the outhouse!' he said, referring to newspaper squares.

However, there were magazines that were not used as toilet paper. For example, the *Bulletin*, the influential Australian magazine founded in 1880, was far too valuable, the *Women's Weekly* was too

Newspaper squares — the 'thrifty dodge' noted by the Prince of Wales's staff member. Things have certainly improved greatly for us in this area. These squares look a lot tougher than what we use now — but much more informative!

smooth and the *Catholic Weekly* was never used, at least by those of that faith.

During hard times, the highest and the lowest in the land had something in common. In 1892 a member of the staff of His Excellency, The Prince of Wales, wrote to the Queen's Secretary from Windsor Castle, noting 'We all admire the various little economical thrifty dodges here. In the WCs — newspaper squares ...'

In sharp contrast to those who used newspaper and tissue, some hardy folk, or those who couldn't afford the luxury of paper in any form, used corn husks and even pumpkin leaves. Children in the affluent modern world find this difficult to believe.

Looking back to the days when paper was not available or was considered far too valuable a commodity to be used for such a lowly task in the privy, other methods were employed. For example, the Romans tied sponges to sticks and used them. In between use the sponges were kept in pots of salt water.

When rolls of toilet paper first became available they were relatively expensive and to have a roll in the toilet was a high status symbol. Many people refused to use it because they could see no point in effectively throwing money down the pit. One story relates how people felt about the new-fangled product. 'As a child I can remember our first roll of toilet paper. We had important visitors coming and Mum decided to buy a roll. It was hung proudly in the loo. After the visitors had gone, Mum discovered that the visitors had not used any so she returned it to the store asking for a refund and saying it was far too expensive to use just for the family!'

The use of toilet paper is on the increase. Millions of tonnes are going down the drain every year and have done so since first introduced in 1871. Toilet paper today has become an important part of privy decor with myriad colours and patterns to choose from and a range of novelty types available. One German manufacturer reproduced Deutschmarks on toilet paper and one British manufacturer printed leading politicians' faces on the rolls.

ENVIRONMENTAL CONSIDERATIONS

From an environmental perspective, some say that the use of coloured and printed paper is far from satisfactory. The bleaching and dyeing processes are not only energy inefficient but the dye products that filter back to the environment cause nothing but harm. Unbleached paper is considered more environmentally friendly and although it may not have the smooth, silky qualities of the refined paper it is quite an improvement on the shiny paper that was once issued to government departments.

Attempts have been made to reduce the amount of paper used in the privy. One device that allows only one square to be torn off per revolution is most frustrating but it achieves its aim, an important factor in times of energy conservation.

The toilet roll holder, like many other privy accessories, is a device with which many inventors have experimented. Rarely used nowadays is a simple piece of string threaded through the centre of the roll; instead, high technology has contributed in this area. One holder even incorporates a radio, which makes it a very flash and functional item!

Many modern toilet roll holders run too freely and children who give an overzealous tug end up with half the roll on the floor. To overcome this problem, Stan Richards of Maitland, who grew up in the thrifty 'newspaper' era, invented a holder that works perfectly. The device incorporates a swinging arm with a weighted roller that runs on top of the toilet roll and applies just enough weight to stop the toilet roll spinning freely.

In the environmentally conscious future it is doubtful that regular toilet paper users will resort to ancient Roman methods or any of the other systems that abound. Perhaps they will eventually adapt to the high technology paperless loos being developed.

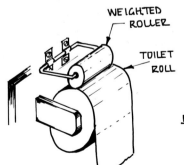

WEIGHTED ROLLER

TOILET ROLL

NON SPINNING TOILET ROLL HOLDER
STAN RICHARDS - MAITLAND

It was only a tiny thing when we planted it! Too much fertiliser, maybe?

Environmental Improvements

There appear to have been two schools of thought when it came to dressing up the outhouse. The 'do nothing' school left the outhouse totally uncared for, an affirmative statement of simple design function; on the other hand, dressing up the outhouse enabled the owners to make a statement about their 'pride and joy'.

THE 'GREENING UP' of the structure did not detract from its usefulness; it simply made it a more pleasant place to visit. It also disguised the building so that it became a more aesthetically acceptable feature of the backyard.

There was a whole range of plants suitable for dressing up the 'little house'. Honeysuckle, wisteria, and from a practical point of view grape, choko, passionfruit and bean vines, depending on climatic conditions, were popular choices. Morning glory, a fast 'cover-up-anything' creeper, was known as the dunny creeper. Climbing roses were used but, generally, thorny vines were not popular as an excursion could be spoilt if one had cause to stumble up the garden path and fall into one. Sanitary men were not too fond of thorny vines, for if they became caught with a full can on their shoulder a disaster could ensue. Many outhouses had privacy shields that provided a trellis for climbing plants. Screens also helped keep the building cool and gave the whole area an aura of being cared for.

Some shields were used for purposes other than for privacy. Famous Australian cricketer Doug Walters is believed to have had a dunny in his backyard and on the wooden privacy shield was painted a set of cricket stumps. Maybe the Australian Cricket Board should preserve this dunny in view of its importance...the starting point of Doug's brilliant cricket career.

Going down the back in some climes was a bone-chilling experience in winter, so any environmental improvements had to take this into consideration. The best location under these conditions was away from trees and buildings that would leave it in shade. In warmer latitudes, conversely, most outhouses were placed under trees or had trees planted next to them. Fruit trees were a popular choice and if the outhouse was a pit type, the used hole often had a tree planted in it after being filled with soil. Fig and mulberry trees seemed to thrive and a sortie down the back could be a very pleasurable activity. Mango trees were not recommended.

One woman recalls. 'I used to hate going to the loo at night when the mangos were ripe. Flying foxes feasting in the tree would drop the fruit on the roof making a frightful racket; meanwhile the cane toads were coming in the door.'

Ornamentals such as maples, jacaranda and pepper trees were popular, especially the latter as some say that the crushed leaves of the peppercorn tree kept the flies at bay and generally brought a pleasant odour to the area.

Any outside loos that remain today are sometimes dressed up in association with festivals and tidy town competitions. Some towns have dressing-up-the-dunny competitions as part of annual celebrations; once again, these are indications of a hankering for the good old days, if there ever was such a thing. However, most people who experienced the days of 'down the back' would not trade their inside water closet for the sanitary arrangements of the past.

Oooops! Easy enough to find, but what can you do once you're there?

Getting There

During the daytime there were usually no problems getting to the loo at the end of the garden path other than being distracted by a neighbour intent on a yarn. However, at night it could be a different matter.

THROWING SOME LIGHT
ON THE SUBJECT

BEFORE BATTERY-POWERED torches became an affordable item, lighting arrangements varied considerably. The cheapest form was a slush lamp, which consisted of nothing more than a jam tin cut down a little and shaped to form a crude reflector. The tin was filled with lard or fat and a wick was kept afloat by a cork or twig. Youngsters sitting in an outhouse on a cold and windy night with a flickering slush lamp aglow would, no doubt, have let their imaginations run to thoughts of ghosts and things that go bump in the night.

This classy loo (in Berkshire, England) even has a candle window — to the left at the top of the doorway — making a night-time trip much more civilised. The loo is built on to the wall to act as a buttress — they think of everything, don't they!

Are there any haunted loos? (As there are cases of murders having been committed in loos it stands to reason that there could be a ghost or two. King James I was murdered in a garderobe.)

Candles were a simple form of lighting. They were placed in a tin attached to the back of the door or in a cut-down bottle. A unique three-candlepower dunny chandelier comprised of old telephone insulators attached to a bullock wagon hub ring was suspended from the roof by a chain. The candles screwed into the internal threads of the insulators, which also caught the drips.

Kerosene lamps had the advantage of lighting the way to the facility on a windy night when a candle or slush lamp would have blown out. Extra light from a kero lamp meant that the intending user could inspect the outhouse for unwelcome visitors like crawlies that hop and glide in the dark.

THINGS THAT GO BUMP IN THE NIGHT

SPIDER WEBS STRUNG across the garden path could create discomfort, and panic bordering on hysteria could overcome youngsters when older children played tricks. One prank that would send young children screaming back to the house involved the use of an old tin and a candle. Holes depicting a face would be punched into the sides of the tin while a lighted candle was pushed through a hole in the bottom; the tin was then hung in a tree. The result resembled a glowing face swinging back and forth, which was enough to scare the most intrepid adventurer.

George and Dick Hill wrote a poem that tells of the problems of going to the loo at night. The poem details how they had to take

Here is just the thing to terrify those visiting the loo at night. There is a hole in the bottom for the candle to be inserted, turning the can into a very convincing ghost, smile or no smile!

their sister to the dunny on a dark night because she had a gastric attack. She walked into the outhouse and let out a terrible howl, for sitting on the seat was a large brown owl. It was not known who received the bigger fright, for the sister rushed out and the owl left a message on the seat.

Another story that describes how frightening it could be for a child to tackle the outhouse at night appeared in the *Australian Women's Weekly* in November 1992, and was written by Glenise Pettersen:

> I awoke from a deep sleep and, needing to use the lavatory, found my way to the back verandah. I flicked on the switch,

which threw a weak light up the path, leaving a shadowy glow to the lav door. The moon was suffocated by dark cloud, and a piercing wind blew dead leaves across the gravel. Staring up the path, I wondered if I really needed to go. I did. So I assured myself there was nothing to be scared of and hurried up the path.

As I stepped through the shadowy door, a deep growl left me spineless and a following snarl had me under the verandah light before I had even been where I was going! I raced for the safety of my bed and buried myself.

The rest of the night was spent in sleepless discomfort.

In the morning, I told Mum about the monster in the lavatory. She told me that I must have had a nightmare!

The next night, the inevitable happened. Again, I needed to use the lav. Close to tears, I forced myself out of bed, telling myself not to be a cry baby.

I turned on the verandah light, armed myself with the straw broom and peered up the shadowy path. Desperate to use the lav, I crept to the side of the dark building and listened.

Silence. I bashed the broom against the wall. Not the slightest sound from inside. Just to make sure, I poked the straw broom around the corner. The broom violently left my hands as it was tugged inside and, too afraid to move, I heard it being thrashed from side to side. Then snarls revived my frozen blood and sent me bellowing for my father.

Sobbing frantically, I told him there was a terrible monster in the lavatory. It was his turn to tell me I was having a nightmare but, to calm me, he said he would show me there was nothing there.

I followed him to the edge of the verandah, but not a step further, and watched him, barefoot and tousle-haired, stagger up the path and disappear around the door. He did not stagger back! Loudly cursing, and clutching the cords of his pyjama pants, he flew past me.

I'd had my eyes so firmly glued to the lavatory they felt as if they were stuck to the weatherboards! Then the creak of the flywire door caught my attention. Father was back; he had loaded his shotgun and, snapping the barrel shut, he cautioned me to be quiet. No statue could have been quieter.

At that moment, the moon decided to defy the clouds and offered its help by shining on my father, on the path and glinting off the gunmetal of the shotgun, as he strode purposefully towards the lavatory.

As I watched, it seemed as if the silent fingers of night pulled at his loosely tied pyjama cords. The pants suddenly fell down around his ankles and sent him flying face first into the dirt.

A deafening blast split the night as the jarred shotgun flew from his hands, discharging both barrels right through the lav roof! Blue and silver sparks danced along the corrugated iron.

I jumped screaming from the floor to an old wooden table that Mum used for her washing. Yowls reverberated from the lavatory, and the black shape of a dog clawed its way over the lattice then streaked across the yard, followed by my father roaring, 'You bloody mongrel!'

The stray dog never returned. And it was lucky for him that he didn't, because what my father was going to do to it, should it come back, is not worth writing about. But, if I ever again wanted to use the lav at night — though I tried desperately not to — I always armed myself with the straw broom, belted it against the lav wall and just to be sure, threw it in before I ventured to enter.

Many times my father relived the story with his mates, embroidering the facts and, amid much laughter, would sing 'The Dog Sits on the Thunderbox'.

Only Mum and I didn't think it was particularly funny.

Cartoon by Will Pearce.

An outhouse with concete road compression test blocks as a fence feature! Broken Hill, NSW.

Attacks
and
Pranks

In Australia, Empire Day (celebrating Queen Victoria's birthday) was traditionally celebrated on 24 May with a bonfire and fireworks. It was on this night that certain anti-social activities were carried out by local larrikins.

PRIME TARGETS ON late night sorties by gangs armed with the most potent fireworks were letterboxes and backyard privies — and more points were gained if the latter was occupied. Blasting someone's letterbox was poor game compared to a successful outhouse raid! The intelligence information concerning adult toilet-going habits was extraordinary and could be pooled by neighbourhood gangs.

Blowing up privies was not only restricted to the young; anybody who fell into disfavour could find their pride and joy destroyed overnight. Such was the method in the old days when one had a score to settle.

Children had an inherent dislike for toilets. Maybe it had something to do with school toilet blocks and dashes across muddy, burr-infested playgrounds, or with the chance that a school bully

The school dunny at Upper Bingara, NSW. Very neat, clean and tidy, and carefully placed just the right distance from the schoolroom. The school may not be modern, but it is certainly in a beautiful spot. And so is its loo!

might be lurking at the toilet block to mete out punishment. Many favours have been given for fear of being thrown in the urinal by a school bully. One old gentlemen said, 'As a child I used to hate the school toilet. It was a frightful place. Better to do a country one than go in there.'

Pranks tested out at home could be further refined at school with the help of playground friends, and these were common occurrences. For students of electricity a very practical experiment in conductivity was to drive two nails into a wooden bench seat in the outhouse so the heads were left slightly raised above the seat. This meant that the nail heads came into contact with bare flesh when the user sat down. Connected to the underside of the nails were two wires that led to an old magneto. At an opportune moment a charge would be delivered, resulting in the occupant making a hasty and somewhat bemused exit.

Another oft-repeated prank was to bombard the dunny with rocks while it was occupied. Children, of course, would not do this to adults but children of the same age or younger were fair game. Yet another prank was to run a stick across the outside of a corrugated iron dunny; the resultant noise inside the loo was deafening and would soon upset the tenant.

Other pranks were too diabolical to mention but those of a milder nature included throwing a paper bag full of water over the top of the door on to the occupant. Outhouses that had an access door at the back so the can could be removed attracted special attention from the mischievous. 'When I went in,' said one lady, 'my brother filled a bike pump with water and squirted me from behind, so when he went in I took the hose and dealt him a good blast.'

Inserting stinging nettles through the access hole was a common prank but one particularly inventive trick was performed by a young lad who placed two nails in the end of a broom handle, point out, snake fang width apart. When his sister went in he jabbed her with it. She ran out of the dunny screaming, 'I've been bitten by a snake.' Her mother inspected the marks and decided on prompt action that meant a 15 kilometre buggy ride to hospital. Of course the poor girl never did show any signs of snake bite even after being kept in hospital for four days. The old gentleman who related this story went on to say, 'I have never told my mother or my sister what I did.'

Cartoon by Will Pearce.

Today's children view these deserted and dilapidated loos of the past as curiosities, not as places to get up to mischief in. No more dangerous pranks, but rather less fun, too. This loo is in Bingara, NSW.

In Sydney back in the 1950s there were a number of open-air movie theatres and one such place had a row of pan dunnies with their rears facing the laneway. Children wanting entrance to the movies without paying would get in 'through the lav'. With a cautious glance over their shoulder, they would open the can access door, pull out the can, crawl in through the door and up through the seat. The last in was responsible for replacing the can and closing the can access door. What kids would do to for a free night at the 'fleas and itches'!

Terrace-style houses sometimes had adjoining outhouses that shared a common cesspit. The dividing wall in some cases did not extend below seat level so children, if they knew the adjoining loo was occupied, would poke their heads down the hole and peer into the gloom to see who was using the loo next door.

This construction method also applied to multi-holer dunnies in schoolyards. Not only did children poke their heads down the hole to see who was at the other end, but they also took a plank, placed it through the seat and 'planked' the adjacent sitters.

One boy, unfortunately for him, 'planked' the teacher by mistake; his punishment was severe. A plank could also be inserted through the can access door at the rear to give the occupant a nasty shock.

Some children did more than poke their heads down the loo.

One boy actually dug a horizontal shaft from his parents' pit dunny into an adjoining property.

Myrtle Thornton of Stockton, New South Wales, recounted this story.

> My parents had a grocery store and, over a period during the Depression of the early 1930s, it was noticed that stock was going missing from the storeroom in the yard at the back of the shop.
>
> The culprit was the boy next door, one of six children, who had dug a tunnel from his pit loo under our fence, to emerge in a pop hole into the storeroom. When questioned about his actions, the boy replied: 'You shouldn't have left the stock down there!'

Children today can still be moved to lament the passing of their loo or to note its role in the family life in verse:

Our Dunny
by Kylie Bettridge, aged 10

We all adored our dunny,
It was really something great.
But when the wind blew it down.
Our hearts were filled with hate.

The playing of tricks around the outhouse was not just restricted to children. One trick played on a new constable taking up duties at Glebe Police Station, Sydney, involved the use of a naked shop-display dummy. Along the back lanes in Glebe the outhouses are situated behind the terrace houses at the bottom of the yard. The new constable was sent to inspect each privy after dark to see all was in order and above board, but, as a joke, colleagues had placed a naked store dummy in one of the loos. The inspection involved securing each door. All went well until he came across the naked body. In the darkness the dummy looked very life-like. The alarmed officer rushed back to the station to make a report. He soon realised he was on the receiving end of a practical joke. The terrace house dunnies referred to in this story are now classified by the National Trust.

The loo may have died but the climbing rose lingers on...

Wildlife

In the traditional outhouse, one was close to nature in more ways than one. Because the 'down the back' was only frequented for short periods, the various forms of wildlife that took up residence could be forgiven for thinking it was abandoned. As a result the outhouse could provide a rich and sometimes not so harmless field of observation for the keen student of nature.

Many kinds of spiders found ceilings, wall frames and dark crevices behind doors excellent spots for setting up house. Louvred windows were also favoured because they provided easy access to hunting opportunities both inside and outside the outhouse. Generally, spiders gave no offence, but exception was taken with the red-back and the large species such as the huntsman and tarantula, which frightened some timid souls. The activities of spiders varied greatly throughout the day and observing them could be quite absorbing. With luck there might be a blowie, a moth or beetle caught in a web, an event always good for a few dramatic moments. Watching a web being spun could also pass the time most pleasantly.

A photo taken at great risk to life and limb! Here is a paperbark wasp nest on a Red River Gum, with wasps about to launch an attack on the unsuspecting passer-by. The gum is, of course, on the way to the loo! The whole dangerous episode took place at Quambone, NSW.

No snakes between the end of this chain and the loo, thank you!

Of all the stinging insects the most ferocious is the paperbark wasp, and even those most sensitive to the natural order of things who try to avoid killing anything would take measures to destroy the nests if they set up home in or near the privy.

Birds also made use of the outhouse, nesting in rafters or any other available nook. They were not encouraged, as having a bird perched above the sitter brought a certain sense of insecurity to the business at hand.

Ants were not a serious problem. They tended to provide a sense of wonderment and provoked questions as to how such small insects could carry a moth many times larger than themselves.

Termites, however, have played a destructive role in the demise of the outhouse. Termites are clever engineers, for they know just how much wood to chew away without the building collapsing. They work away quietly without apparent effect for years, and then suddenly one day you walk into the outhouse and almost fall through the floor.

Termites have not been the only factor in the demise of the 'down the back'. Storms and tempests have blown many a loo over, some while being occupied. This happened to one lady of the house in the village of Limbri near Tamworth in New South Wales, while she was attending to a call of nature. Unfortunately, the storm caused the outhouse to collapse and the door to fall inwards, making it extremely difficult to extricate the poor soul trapped inside. To eliminate the problem of total collapse the experts advise that one corner post of the dunny should be sunk well into the ground.

SNAKE ENCOUNTERS

SNAKES, IT SEEMS, were the most feared forms of wildlife to have in or around the loo, and stories abound of people being bailed up. One childhood experience reported to me was truly frightening. After inspecting the outhouse for danger a little girl placed her kerosene lamp on the floor. Shortly afterwards a king brown, one of the most deadly of Australian snakes, came in the door. She immediately jumped up onto the bench seat and to her surprise the snake ignored her completely and curled around the base of the kerosene

Obviously, not a loo for anyone or anything that is not a bird! It's such a lovely sign, too —
what a pity the loo doesn't really match it!

lamp. It was obviously only interested in keeping warm. Still, there she was with a snake between her and the doorway. What was she to do? She called for her father, who soon dispatched the intruder. As they used to say, it's moments like these you need Minties!

All parents know when a child's scream is fair dinkum. Children let out the most shrilling scream when confronted with a snake. One little boy called Tim ventured to the outhouse one day and as he was about to enter he noticed a very large snake hanging from the roof. The ensuing scream brought Dad and Mum running. Fortunately for the snake it escaped down a rabbit burrow, but it took Tim a long while to venture down the back on his own again.

Many snake encounters, as was the case with Tim, were due to the bad location of the privy. The dunny in question was next to the chicken coop. Even though it was a pleasure to watch the activities of the chooks while attending to nature, outhouses in this location attracted snakes as a matter of course. Chicken feed attracted rodents and rodents attracted snakes. Farm dogs were, on occasions, tied up next to the privies as a means of deterring snakes.

A delightful wildlife story by Bert Facey in his remarkable memoirs *A Fortunate Life* concerns his foster mother and is most evocative of farm life in the first decade of this century:

> Mum had an arrangement to give us an idea when it was lunchtime. She would peg a white tea towel on the clothes line near the house at ten minutes to midday. By the time we got home and had a clean up, lunch would be ready.
>
> One day, at the signal, we started walking towards the house. We were about fifty yards away when we heard Mum let out a terrible scream. She came running out of the lavatory holding up her dress with one hand and clutching her bottom with the other. She was yelling out loudly, 'I've been bitten by a snake!' Frank and I ran to her and helped her inside the

house. Frank took her into the bedroom, and told me to run over to the Connors' place and get Jack to bring his horse and sulky to take Mum to the doctor. It was a little over two miles to Jack's and I ran all the way. It was a very hot day and I was done in when I got there. It took me a few minutes before I could explain what had happened.

Jack wasn't long putting the horse in the sulky and we drove back. Mum was crying when we got there. Frank told Jack that the snake bite was very distinct and he had cut it with his razor and sucked out as much blood as he could.

Mum looked very pale and was badly shocked. After giving me some quick instructions as to what to do while they were away, they set out to get Mum to the doctor in Narrogin as soon as possible. Jack's sulky horse was a beauty, one of the best in the district and although Frank and Jack were at loggerheads over the bore, they had forgotten about it with the crisis in hand. The trip to Narrogin would take them all afternoon and well into the night.

After they had gone I got a nice handy stick, about four feet long, and went into the lavatory after the snake. This lavatory was mainly used by Mum; I never used it and Frank only sometimes. It was made of galvanised iron and had a small hole cut out at the back to allow Mum to slide the pan in. (The pan was an old kerosene tin cut off to fit.) A bag was hung on to the back wall to cover the hole. With the stick I approached the lavatory, carefully looking in and around, but I couldn't see any sign of the snake. I lifted the bag up very slowly (I was scared stiff), then I heard something move. Quickly I dropped the bag and jumped back. Then all was quiet again. I lifted the bag once more. This time I noticed some feathers, and as I lifted the bag further, more feathers came into view. All at once I knew what had bitten Mum. It wasn't a snake and all my fears turned to mirth. In fact, I almost lost control of myself with laughing.

Mum's snake was a hen. The hen had made a nest close to the pan to lay her eggs and Mum hadn't noticed her. She didn't mind Mum sitting on the lavatory at first, but when she went broody — a hen can be placid while laying and vicious when broody — she had decided to peck Mum on the bottom.

Mum was very frightened of snakes and also terribly frightened of dingoes. She wouldn't venture outside on her own, except in special circumstances.

They were away for nearly four days. When they came home Mum seemed jolly and didn't show any ill effects from the shock she'd had. I asked her how she was and she said that the doctor had said that he didn't think it was a snake that had bitten her and if it was it wasn't poisonous. She asked if I'd looked around the lavatory for the snake and I said that I had and that I had found the thing that had bitten her. I said that it was still in the lavatory and offered to show it to her.

We went to the lavatory and I lifted up the bag. She looked under and exclaimed, 'Good God, no!' She said that the doctor had said that it looked like beak marks but it never occurred to her that a hen might have done it. She stood for a while and seemed to be thinking, or working something out in her mind. Then suddenly she said, 'Did you have any visitors while we were away or see anyone?' I said, 'No.' 'Well,' she said, 'don't you say anything, not even to Frank or anybody about this. If you do I'll be the laughing stock of the district.' She said, 'Bert, I love you, but if you tell anyone about this I'll kill you.' I promised not to tell anyone. Nothing more was said about the 'snake bite'.

Even today snakes can be a problem in the modern facility. Imagine going into the WC and looking into the bowl to find the tail of a baby black snake hanging down from inside the inner lip of the bowl. One's first reaction is to pull the chain, but with a septic system the snake is flushed into the tank. One householder did pull the chain; the ensuing problem was that no one would use the toilet until the exact location of the snake was known. What if it

Cartoon by Will Pearce

reappeared at some inopportune time? The men of the house, of course, were called to deal with the matter. They removed the inspection cover and discharged the four-ten, a small-gauge shotgun that many women on properties keep handy to dispatch unwanted intruders, into the tank, which put an end to the matter.

Problems with snakes in the toilet also occur in other countries. A story that appeared in the *Washington Post* in 1992 tells of an encounter one young girl had when visiting the 'bathroom'. 'Lawyers Attempt to Get Snake Down Toilet Bowl in Courtroom Demonstration' read the headline. On 21 July 1991 a nine-year-old girl went to the bathroom of her Ottawa apartment and discovered, in the toilet, a large python. The girl told her mother who called the authorities; they managed to catch the snake. ('We have this toilet surrounded. Come out with your hands up.') It was determined that the snake belonged to a man in an upstairs apartment; in an attempt to get rid of his pet he had flushed the snake down the toilet, causing the snake to suffer abrasions and what the article described as 'a bad case of pneumonia'. The prosecutor charged the owner with cruelty to animals. The defence lawyer, determined to have the case thrown out of court, actually had a water-filled toilet bowl brought into the courtroom in an attempt to prove that the snake would willingly dive down the toilet of its own accord. In fact the snake chose not to dive down the toilet and the defendant was found guilty.

One of my ceramic scultpures of a dunny — a redback spider's delight!

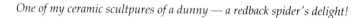

This isolated outback dunny would make an ideal home for many types of native fauna!

A rather classy public hall loo, all iron plus electric light!

Festival Time

Throughout Australia the outhouse has been the subject of numerous festivals and celebrations. Its public profile has been raised to extraordinary heights and, in the process, a lot of people have had fun and, most importantly, a considerable amount of money has been raised for worthwhile organisations.

THE LOCAL LIONS CLUB in Tongala, near Echuca in northern Victoria, turned the advent of the sewerage connection into a massive folk festival that won nationwide media coverage. The 'Burn the Dunny Festival' ran for two days and involved thousands of people in a staggering range of activities that climaxed with the ceremonial burning of a dunny on the village green. The town's former sanitary man, Ray Gay of Yackandandah, wasn't forgotten in the celebrations. Ray was given the honour of igniting the dunny as a navy bugler played 'The Last Post'.

There was a dunny ball, where five hundred people danced to music played by a Royal Australian Navy Band; a dunny cram with some twenty-nine children packing into an outhouse; and novelty sporting events such as unrolling a toilet roll and threading it through a toilet seat, as well as toilet roll tossing. The main event was a 120-metre dash with a half-filled dunny can over a hazardous obstacle course. By the time the ashes of the sacrificed dunny were cold, the Lions Club had raised $8000 for the Anti-Cancer Council of Victoria.

Grahame Watt, a local bush poet of Kyabram near Tongala, was at the festival and was moved to write:

The Burning of the Loo

We've bought a brand new toilet,
With a button you can press.
The water falls in torrents,
And it sparkles — more or less.

All chromium and tiled out
(Inside the house at last!)
But the old folk feel nostalgia,
And think of days gone past.

We'll miss our outside 'dunny'
With the splintery seat so hard,
That little house we knew so well,
Down the bottom of the yard.

It had a sort of lean on,
And was propped to keep it right,
Dad laughed and said 'It's caused by
The wind that blows at night.'

The door it had a patent lock
That was never known to fail.
It had a strap of leather,
Which you hooked up on a nail.

There were little squares of paper,
All hanging on a string
Hours of top class reading,
If you liked that sort of thing.

It used to have a knot-hole,
In the side wall by the seat.
If you turned your head and closed one eye
You'd see right up the street.

You'd walk down in the darkest night
A kero lamp as guide,
And inspect the 'dyke' for danger
Cracks where snakes and spiders hide.

Then deep in meditation
Your thoughts would be upset.
For a voice would interrupt you —
'Have you finished down there yet?'

Now we've lost our dear old nightman,
And his story's sad to tell.
He's really out of business —
Things haven't panned out well!

So spare a thought for that 'little house',
As you flush your pan so new,
And shed a tear for good times gone,
With the 'Burning of the Loo'.

In the broad scheme of things it is not so important that the days are numbered for the good old 'down the back', but as Grahame's poem states, old folk feel nostalgia and a yearning for the good old days.

A few weeks before the Tongala spectacular, the city of Gosford, north of Sydney, discovered the appeal of the dunny as a folk festival attraction. As part of Gosford's annual springtime 'Festival of the Waters', a dunny race was staged. It was a fringe activity and no one really expected that it would appeal to many people, particularly as it was competing with a stunning range of cultural and sporting events. To the great delight of the organisers almost three thousand people turned out to cheer the eighteen mobile dunnies competing in the Sorbent Great Trot. Teams of three had to pull or push their outhouses on wheels over a 500-metre course with a fourth member sitting inside. A professional race caller was recruited to call the race and the local media gave in-depth coverage from every angle, including a broadcast form guide and betting guide. Gosford became known as the dunny racing capital of the world.

Another activity that uses the outhouse as a fund-raiser is the 'dunny dip'. Small, inexpensive gifts are wrapped and placed in a dunny can, and then for a monetary donation the participants take a dip which involves plunging their hands down through the seat hole and into the can to retrieve a gift. The dunny is dressed up with props including model red-back spiders and snakes as well as other items such as newspaper squares and lamps that would have been found in the good old 'down the back'.

Some tidy town competitions have in some ways assisted in the demise of some of Australia's not-so-grand buildings, including the outhouse. However, where dunnies have not been demolished they have become part of the dressing-up of the town. In some places prizes are awarded for the best-maintained loo.

*A home for old loos? The loo scrapheap? Out of work loos? Loos on parade? The loo zoo?
No, actually old fishermen's loos at Cam's Wharf, NSW.*

Literary Notes, Cartoons, and Song

There is not an area of the media or the arts that has not used the folklore associated with the loo to entertain or get a message across. Many songs have outhouses mentioned in their lyrics, dunny business is a cartoonist's delight, and stories about dunnies keep appearing in magazines and newspapers. It's as though the editors instruct their journalists to 'write a dunny story' when there is little to do or give it as an assignment to a new 'chum'.

Memorial to the Dead Dunny

There you stood
Of iron and wood
The sign in every neighbourhood
That once was culture, once was grace
Refinement of the human race.

Oh noble dunny
Now thought funny
Victim of the times and money
But now, alas, you're gone for good
The Hills Hoist stands where you once stood.

Your life is stilled
Your pit is filled
And lawns now grow where once we thrilled
To read a book, and think a bit
Our daily chance to have a sit.

Old wooden floor
Serrated door
And corrugated iron that wore
The signs of time, the tinge of rust
Proclaiming: 'Once a day — or bust.'

No sexist you
Nor racist too
And Liberal and Labour knew
It mattered not, they heard your call
And you received them, one and all.

But now we see
By law's decree
You're lost to all posterity
For who can worship plastic seat
That's listed in the ads 'en-suite'.

So long ago
And few now know
We old ones with get up and go
Still drift outside and would not miss
The chance of some nostalgic bliss.

'Memorial to the Bush Dunny' from *The Slim Book of Bush Verse* written by the late Rob Charlton.

Going . . .

going . . .(photo courtesy of Stan Dodgson)

The End of an Era — 'Been there dunny that'!   *gone.*

Bibliography

THERE HAVE BEEN many books written on the subject of privyology. Some are serious academic works; others deal in a light-hearted way with folklore and history. The most authoritative and interesting are listed below.

Harington, Sir John, *Metamorphosis of Ajax,* **1596.** 'Ajax' was a pun on 'jakes', which was a slang word used for lavatory. Harington designed the first water closet in 1589. One of his creations was installed in Richmond Palace, the home of Queen Elizabeth I.

Reyburn, Wallace, *Flushed with Pride,* **1969.** This is a biography of one of England's greatest sanitary engineers, Sir Thomas Crapper.

Sale, Chic, *The Specialist,* **1929.** Chic, an American, included a strange monologue in this hilarious book and became a popular after-dinner speaker, often opening with: 'Gentlemen, you are face to face with the champion privy builder of Sangamon County'.

Rose, Rob, *Muddled Meanderings in an Outhouse,* **1970.** This is a popular US anthology now in its fifteenth reprint.

Barlow, Ronald S., *The Vanishing American Outhouse.* This describes in detail all aspects of American dunny business.

Johansen, Swea, *Hemligaus* **(*Our Secret*).** A delightful treasury of stories relating to European and Scandinavian privies.

Baglin, Douglas, *Dinkum Dunnies.* The Australian photographer's book of loos and their idiosyncrasies.

And finally, there is my own previous publication, *Down the Back,* a collection of stories relating to the folklore associated with the Aussie dunny.